CYBERSECURITY

*LEARN INFORMATION
TECHNOLOGY SECURITY:
HOW TO PROTECT YOUR
ELECTRONIC DATA FROM
HACKER ATTACKS WHILE
YOU ARE BROWSING THE
INTERNET WITH YOUR SMART
DEVICES, PC OR TELEVISION*

ALAN GRID

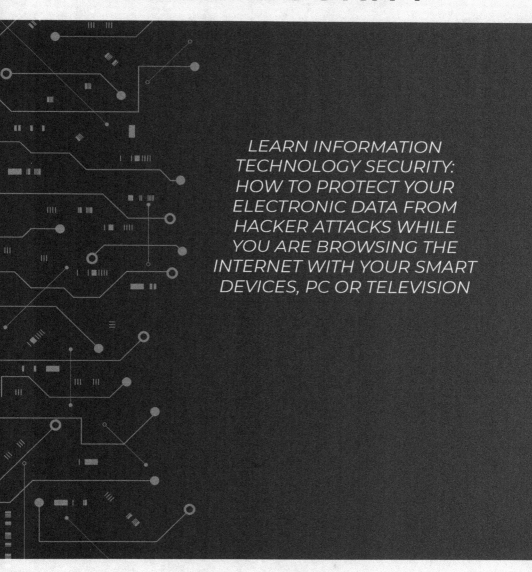

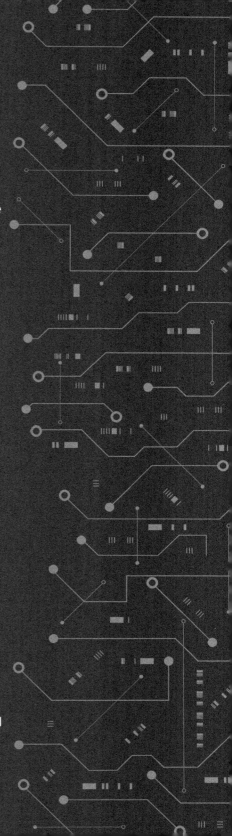

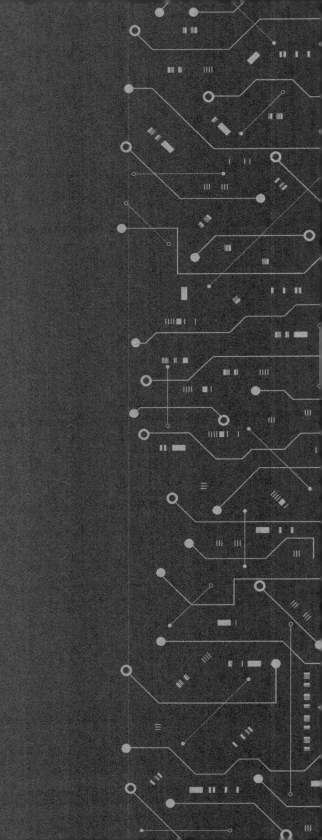

TABLE OF CONTENTS

CHAPTER - 3

CONCLUSION 121

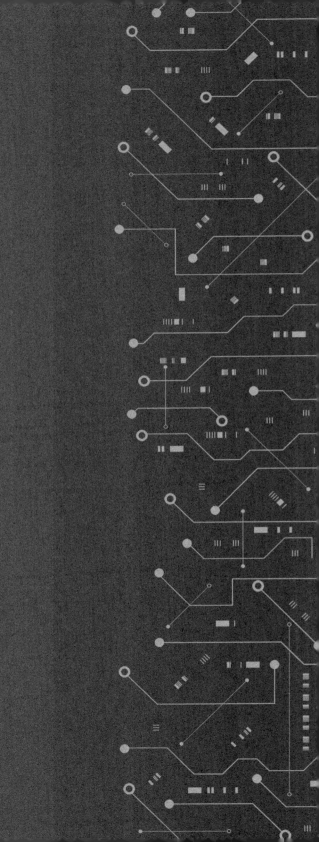

INTRODUCTION

Computer technology has evolved in unimaginable sophistication and innovation ever since its inception. The majority of the advancements, reach, and the power of the internet has aided the popularity of information technology. Today, almost any industry or individual uses computer systems and networks for some purpose or another.

The measures that are taken to protect computer systems, networks and devices against cyber-attacks are categorized as cybersecurity. Although computer technology has evolved leaps and bounds, the same can't be said about cybersecurity.

Cyber-attacks have become increasingly complex and deceptive, with highly skilled cyber-criminals dedicating enormous amounts of time, resources, and energy into launching serious cyber-attacks. However, the means for protecting individuals and organizations from such attacks have been slow to catch up.

Various security measures are discussed at length, including the proper use of passwords and PINs, creating routine back-ups, practicing caution when connecting to public networks, and much more. The discussion also includes how to put those countermeasures into effect without affecting one's lifestyle, productivity, and budget.

The internet has changed the way companies do business. Computers and networks have changed many processes of businesses from manufacturing, operations, communications to finance, distribution, marketing, and customer service. It is common to find the presence of the use of computer systems and the internet in almost all processes related to businesses in one way or another.

The advancements in computer technology, cheaper hardware, and the popularity of the internet have paved the way for the next big thing in technology: The Internet of Things. Objects that used to be "dumb" and needed human intervention have been made "smart" by giving such objects the ability to collect and transmit data and respond to remote commands. The Internet of Things is predicted to continue to grow rapidly while changing the daily lives of humans and the operations of businesses.

IoT devices connect to the internet to perform their duties. As a result, they have been targeted by cyber-attacks with varying motives. The fact that IoT is a relatively novel technology means that IoT devices are yet to be equipped with cybersecurity measures that computers feature. Furthermore, IoT devices are used to carry out demanding duties, including access control and aiding in healthcare.

What is Cyber Security?

The protection of a computer system or network from the adverse effects such as theft or damages to the computer hardware, Software, data, or the services provided by those elements is known as cybersecurity. Cybersecurity is also known as Computer Security and IT Security (Information Technology Security). The field of cybersecurity has fast evolved over the years due to the rapid increase in the use and reliance on the internet, computers, and wireless networks.

The use of devices that are also prone to cyber-attacks such as smart mobile phones, smart televisions, and devices falling under the category of the "Internet of Things" (IoT) has also contributed to the need for the rapid evolution of cybersecurity. The technology and politics that surround the use of the internet, computers, networks, and smart devices are complex that pose many challenges to the world of cybersecurity.

Due to the fast-changing nature of technology

and other factors, cybersecurity is always evolving. Cybersecurity approaches, tools, risk management methods, technologies, best practices, and training are always changing as a result. Threats to cybersecurity also advance with the evolution of technology and the use of devices, Software, and networks that are prone to those threats. Many organizations and even individuals put high levels of emphasis on cybersecurity to protect their valuable hardware, Software, data, services, and organizational objectives.

Cybersecurity has been a huge focus for businesses due to the risk of data breaches that can cripple them in many ways. Such breaches often lead to the loss of highly sensitive data that costs companies their revenues, competitive advantage, reputation, and consumer trust. A data breach is estimated to cost a company around $3.6 million, making cybersecurity a high priority for any business.

Cyber Attacks and Vulnerabilities

A weakness in the design, implementation, internal control, or the operations of a computer, hardware, smart device, Software, or a network results in the exposure to cyber-attacks. The Common Vulnerabilities and Exposures is a database that documents such known vulnerabilities to cyber threats. At least one active attack or an exploit that exists is called an exploitable vulnerability. Various manual and automated tools are used to identify vulnerabilities to cyber-attacks.

When it comes to computers and networks, attacks largely attempt to expose, disable, alter, steal, destroy, or gain access to the use of assets. Any such offensive maneuver that tries to target computer systems, networks, infrastructures, and personal devices can be called a cyber-attack. A cyber-attack can be carried out by an individual or a group with malicious intent putting hardware, data, and functionalities at risk.

Cyber-attacks can be categorized as cyber warfare or cyberterrorism, depending on the nature of the attack and its threat. Furthermore, cyber-attacks can be carried out by various societies and sovereign states operating in anonymity. During a cyberattack, susceptible systems and devices are hacked into while achieving the malicious intents of the attacker or the attackers. The scale of a cyberattack may also vary from a single computer, device, individual, or company is the primary target to infrastructures of entire nations.

Information Security Culture

The behavior of employees plays a key role in establishing cybersecurity in companies. Changes and improvements of a company's culture and practices can help employees effectively work towards achieving information security. Employees sometimes do not realize that they are an integral part of a company's effort towards achieving satisfactory levels of cybersecurity. Their actions may sometimes not align with the cybersecurity goals of a company as a result.

A company should continuously make improvements to its information security culture while making sure that employees understand the role they need to play. The process is never-ending with an ongoing cycle of change, evaluation, and maintenance. The five steps involved in managing a company's information security culture are pre-evaluation, strategic planning, operative planning, implementing, and post-evaluation.

Pre-evaluation brings awareness regarding the company's current information security culture and policy while highlighting behavior that might make it vulnerable against cyber threats. The next step in the process, which is strategic planning, then creates a program towards increasing awareness with a clear target to achieve as a company. Operative planning involves working towards a better culture by improving internal communication, security awareness, and training.

Implementing is a step that consists of four phases, which are the commitment of management, communication with employees, providing courses for employees, and the commitment of the employees. Managers first commit to implementing better information security practices within the company and then communicates the company's intentions to the employees. Then the employees are provided with education and training regarding information security.

Finally, the employees of the company committed to bringing about an improved and satisfactory information security culture. The final step, which is Post-Evaluation, assesses how well the planning and implementation went and identifies any areas that remain to be unresolved.

Systems That Are Vulnerable to Cyber-Attacks

The number of individuals, businesses, and organizations relying on computer systems has grown rapidly. It has resulted in increasing the number of systems that are at risk of cyber-attacks. Such vulnerable entities are scattered across various industries, with almost all industries out there being vulnerable at different levels.

Financial Systems

Computer systems belonging to financial institutions and regulators have a high risk of being targeted by hackers. The U.S. Securities and Exchange Commission, investment banks, and commercial banks are prime targets of hackers seeking illicit gains and market manipulation. Furthermore, any website or mobile application that store or accept credit card numbers, bank account information, and brokerage accounts are also under the risk of being hacked.

Hackers and hacker groups take a high interest in attacking the networks and websites of such institutions since they can enjoy immediate financial spoils by making purchases, transferring money, and selling acquired data to interested parties in the black market. ATMs and in-store payment systems have also been targeted by hackers who aim to gather customer PIN codes and account details.

Dark Web

The dark web sounds scary and almost sends shivers down the spine of most people. The dark web is well-known for harboring illegal activity that lots of people don't want to engage in. The question starts spinning in our heads that if the dark web is a place for illegal activity, then why does it exist in the first place and who allows it to run without any kind of restrictions. Is there any purpose behind the existence and flourishing of the dark web, or is the place being handled by a strong bunch of lot? There are three major parts of the internet known as the deep web, surface web, and dark web. Let me discuss each type individually and in detail.

The surface web consists of around ten percent of the entire internet, and it includes things such as Google and other search engines. You can use keywords to search for different things to read, sell, or buy. Then comes the deep web that is the place where you can store the information that is unavailable to most users. This includes things that you have protected by a password such as a bank account subscription services as well as certain medical information. A majority of the webspace consists of this type of information. The third spot belongs to the dark web that is not accessible by a standard internet user. You cannot access this webspace through Firefox, Opera, and Google Chrome, and it can have any kind of information. The word dark is attributed to this web space because of its limited accessibility.

You might be wondering if the dark web is completely illegal for a common user. Thankfully, the answer is no. Mere entering the dark web doesn't count as an illegal activity, but what you do in the dark web can be categorized as legal or illegal. You can access the dark web through Tor anonymous browser. You can download it just like Google Chrome and Firefox. The difference is that it works in a different manner. You have to travel through different overlay networks when you are using Tor or The Onion Router. Just like an onion, it has a number of layers to pass through. The speed of Tor is usually slower than other browsers. If you can get your hands on a Virtual Private Network, it is better to ensure maximum security.

To clear the longstanding confusion, Tor is not a dark web but a tool to access the dark web. Also, Tor can be used to access general webspace such as Google and Yahoo, and your travel through the surface web will be more secure. Rather than a place for illegal activities, the dark web is considered as a place for a high level of online privacy. You can buy illegal drugs through on the dark web and get them delivered to your postal address without giving anyone a hint to what was in the package. The ultimate objective to achieve by using dark web depends on what you need, whether you are ready to take the risk of committing an illegal act.

Residents of countries such as Iran where the government control over the internet is touching extreme levels, the dark web becomes a necessity. Residents from these countries access Facebook and Twitter through the dark web. They log into their onion versions that have been officially launched for users who are subjected to censorship.

CHAPTER - 1

COMMON CYBERATTACKS

Cyberattacks are getting highly sophisticated as hackers are coming up with the latest and innovative methods to stage an attack and threaten the security of different computer networks. The attacks are getting so much sophisticated that they are getting tougher to detect. Consequently, the attacks are getting more lethal than they were ever before.

Cybersecurity doesn't depend on the size of your organization. Whether you have a start-up business or a multimillion-dollar company, you should be able to be aware of how risky a cyberattack can be. The rise of cyberattacks gives room to the question of why do hackers attack a cyberspace? What is the motivation behind such heinous attacks? A general perception is that financial gain drives them to stage high profile cyberattacks on the computer systems of big corporations. Some also do that for espionage purposes. This chapter will shed light on the motivations that hackers have on their backs to penetrate an individual computer or an enterprise computer.

Most of the time, the attack is a kind of breach that aims at infiltrating the credit and debit card details. This information is then sold on the dark web later on to bag heavy profit. The story doesn't end here. In a majority of cases, profit is just a smokescreen to hide something bigger and deeper.

Espionage is also linked to a breach of data of a corporation or an official website of a country. These kinds of attacks typically are aimed at retrieving information from the victim. There are lots of things that remain the same when it comes to espionage through a cyberattack, including monitoring of communication running on the cyberspace. There is another popular technique in espionage known as stealing secrets. Earlier on, this task came into the domain of individuals who physically penetrated the space and compromised certain assets that are found inside the organization. To give you a taste of how it all happened, I'll state an example from Hollywood. If you are a fan of Tom Cruise and his spy thrillers, you might for sure be acquainted with the character of Ethan, who was always on some kind of mission to infiltrate a facility and steal some important documents that could turn the tables on the bad guys. Spy is the word that they use for such kind of person. Nowadays, things are different. There is hardly anything left in the physical domain. The craft of stealing an important bunch of information is more about being electric. Computers have the capacity to consume billions of files that were once stored in the company's ledgers and on loads of papers.

Espionage

Espionage attacks are getting more sophisticated nowadays. Most of them are state-sponsored or are financed by the corporate sector. Some professional groups act as independent contractors to spy for profit. Espionage is considered as a secretive activity in which attackers formulate a plan to avoid detection and achieve their objectives of collecting important information about the targeted company or individual. Spies are the most persistent attackers who keep on working until they achieve their objective. They keep on trying a number of techniques until they accomplish their mission. Even if they are detected, they don't stop their activities and go on until the completion of the mission.

In most cases, the initial worker is indirect, such as a trusted third-party in the form of an employee who has access to the computer system you want to target. Once the attacker has access inside the system, he will have to move through the systems of the organization and also make his way to the data stores of the company. If you are running a financial consultancy firm, the most important data should be informed about your company's clients.

Once the attacker has access to the documents, he will be in a position to blackmail you.

Profit

The second most common motivation of a hacker is financial gains. They aim at making heavy profits by the attack. The methods of profit-driven attackers vary. Usually, if the data stolen pertains to credit card and debit card details, it is understood that the objective of the cybercrime is financial gain. The information cybercriminals steal afterward sold on the dark web to make a hefty profit. This is the greatest motivator in today's world in which locating the net worth of everyone is so easy. The transparency in financial transactions and details makes money as the single most important objective of a cyberattack. Everyone needs money, and no shortage of cybercriminals wouldn't hesitate to share a pie from the money.

Different hackers use different types of methods that lead to some monetary gain. Cybercriminals use a wide range of methods using financial malware such as Dridex, Shifu, Carbanak, and Rovnix to siphon off loads of swag from the bank accounts of the victim. Another method to rob victims is to by using ransomware such as Tesla. Denial of service attacks (DDoS) is another profit-motivated attack that has become pretty top-notch in popularity over the past years.

Whether you are the owner of a consultancy firm or

a retailer of clothes, you are at a high risk of a serious cyber threat if you conduct your transactions online. They are always after user and financial details that could lead him to the source of your finances as well as your customers' finances. If they loot you, you are devastated because you will not have precious capital to hold grounds. If they loot your customers, you will lose your hard-earned reputation in the market that is equally devastating for your business. In both ways, you are at great risk of losing your business. Attackers, at the height of rage, can use a malware that can target your point of sale (POS) systems.

Sometimes, profit alone is the sole objective of an attacker. For example, your company has secured a contract from the Pentagon to produce sophisticated weapons, and you are on your way to producing them. Hackers can target your company's database to compromise sensitive information that can be of strategic and police use of the attacker. The attacker can be a country that needs this strategic information to update her defense assets. It can be used by politicians to shape up their political campaigns. The chances are high that the state sponsors this kind of attack. Usually, states conduct this kind of classified mission through state-backed resources, but sometimes lack of resources can come in their way, and they have to outsource this kind of mission to experts. Let's take a look at the most breached industries across the world.

Virtually all business is at a considerable risk of a cyberattack, but some industries seem to be more vulnerable to these cyberattacks than the rest of the lot. The type of data that these companies hold makes them more vulnerable to cyberattacks. The very first industry on the line is the health industry.

Health

The health sector tops the list of cyberattacks in the United States, and there are some valid reasons for that. The health sector carries personal information such as names, addresses, information about the income of people, social security numbers, and email IDs. Hackers break into the databases at hospitals and access this information to exploit it later on. Their mode of attack is to gain a kind of unauthorized access to medical programs and an effort to get prescription drugs. Most of the threat has its origins inside the organization while some of the attacks are due to some kind of human error such as leakage of information about a patient by an employee of the hospital. The employee might not have suspected that the information could be manipulated by an individual or an organization.

Public Sector

The second vulnerable sector is public administration. Public administration, such as government departments carry details about the employees, such as names, addresses, bank account numbers, and other personal information that can be compromised and misused if it comes in the hands of bad guys. Another reason why hackers highly target the public sector is that it suffers from a lack of funding in the cybersecurity realm that makes it weak and a potential target of cybercriminals. Personal information of high-ups and confidential information is at the top of the list of a hacker's to-do chart. Confidential information can be sold on the dark web for a heavy price. It can also be sold to a state for bigger profits.

Financial Sector

The financial sector is another field that is most vulnerable to cyberattacks. Hackers relish at the personal information of the owners of hefty bank accounts. In addition, they can lay their hands on the credit card information of the clients of a finance firm.

Food Sector

The food industry is also in the line of industries that can be at great risk of cyberattacks. These businesses are quite vulnerable to certain breaches because they are always collecting credit card details of their customers, and their names and addresses. Once stolen, a hacker can use this precious information to steal the identity of a customer and gain unauthorized access to bank accounts.

CHAPTER - 2
CYBERSECURITY

Types of Cybersecurity

Does it seem that everything now depends on computers as well as the internet? Entertainment, communication, transportation, medicine, shopping, etc. Even banking institutions operate the company online of theirs.

The realization that many the planet is dependent on the internet should encourage us to challenge ourselves.

- Simply just how much of the lifetime of mine is driven by the net?

- Simply just how much of the private info of mine is stored on the web?

- Simply just how much of the company of mine is accessible over networks?

- Simply just how much of my customers' information is accessible over networks?

With these a remarkable dependence on computer systems, neglecting the possibility of cybercrime in the company of yours is incredibly risky & likely bad for you, your business, your employees, together with the buyers of yours.

Without a feeling of security, the company of yours is operating at extremely high risk for cyber-attacks.

Below are numerous kinds of cybersecurity you need to become mindful of. This could help you construct a good foundation for an excellent security strategy.

1. Critical infrastructure security

Important infrastructure safety includes the cyber-physical methods which fashionable societies rely on.

Common examples of essential infrastructure:

- Power grid
- Drinking h2o purification
- Site visitors' lights

Going shopping centers hospitals having the infrastructure of an energy grid on the internet leads to it being prone to cyber-attacks.

Companies with responsibility for any essential infrastructures must do due diligence to realize the vulnerabilities and defend the company of theirs against them. The protection, in addition to the resilience of this essential infrastructure, is crucial to our society's wellbeing and safety.

Companies that are not responsible for the infrastructure that is vital that; however, rely on it for a portion of the company of theirs, should certainly develop a contingency plan by analyzing precisely how an assault on essential infrastructure they rely on might affect them.

2. Application security

You have to choose application protection as among the selection of should have security methods adopted to protect the devices of yours. Software safety uses Software and hardware treatments to tackle outdoors threats, which can form in the development stage of an application.

Apps are a great deal much more accessible over networks, resulting in the adoption of safeguard steps through the development phase to be an imperative stage of the endeavor.

Types of Application security:

Antivirus programs

Firewalls encryption exhibits: These helps to ensure that unauthorized access is stayed away from. Companies likewise could detect extremely vulnerable specifics assets and protect them by certain system security procedures put on these data sets.

3. Network security

As cybersecurity is all about outside threats, community security guards against unauthorized intrusion of the respective inner networks of yours due to malicious goal.

Community security guarantees which internal networks are protected by preserving the infrastructure and inhibiting access to it.

In order to enable you to far better management group security monitoring, security teams currently use machine learning to flag unusual guests, in addition, to alert to threats on time, which is genuine. Network administrators keep on applying policies and procedures to prevent unauthorized access, modification, and exploitation of the system.

Common examples of community protection implementation:

- Extra logins
- Revolutionary passwords
- System security
- Antivirus programs
- Antispyware software
- Encryption
- Firewalls Monitored internet access

4. Cloud security

Enhanced cybersecurity is of all the main reasons the cloud is recording over.

Cloud protection is a software program-based protection tool which protects as well as monitors the info in the cloud materials of yours. Cloud providers are continually producing & utilizing brand new security tools to help enterprise users better secure information of theirs.

The misconception flying about cloud computing is its less secure compared to standard tactics. People will probably believe that the information of yours is much safer when stored on physical methods as well as the servers you've and influence. Nevertheless, it has been established by cloud security that command does not mean security in addition to accessibility matters a lot more than the physical location of the information of yours.

Alert's Logic Cloud Security Report found that on premises environment computer customers experience many more incidents than those of service provider environments.

The statement further finds that

Service provider environment customers experienced an average of 27.8 attacks.

Cloud computing security is comparable to conventional on-premise information centers, simply without the time in addition to the expense of maintaining big data facilities, and also, the risk of security breaches is reduced.

4. Internet of things (IoT) security

IoT details several non-critical as well as crucial cyber actual physical strategies, like appliances, sensors, televisions, Wi-Fi routers, printers, and security cameras.

Based upon Bain & Company's prediction

The combined marketplaces of IoT will create approximately 1dolar1 520 billion in 2021; a lot more than double the 1dolar1 235 billion invested in 2017.

IoT's info center, analytics, consumer devices, networks, legacy embedded approaches & connectors will be the primary engineering of the IoT market.

IoT solutions are usually posted a vulnerable state and in addition, provide hardly any to no security patching. This poses unique security challenges for all those users.

5. Information security

This describes the shelter of information and data from theft, unauthorized access, breaches, etc. to uphold user privacy and also quit identity theft.

6. Disaster recovery

This requires preparing and strategizing to enable

companies to recuperate from cybersecurity/IT disasters. This requires a risk assessment, analysis, prioritizing, and make catastrophe response in addition to recovery methods ready to go. This allows organizations to recuperate quicker from disasters and lower losses.

7. Website security

This is utilized to stop as well as protect websites from cybersecurity risks on the internet. Alternate website protection plans are planning to discuss the website's information source, applications, source codes, and files. Typically, there carries a frequent rise in the volume of data breaches on websites of the past few years, leading to identity thefts, downtime, financial losses, loss of track record in addition to brand image, etc. The main reason for this goes on to become the misconception amongst website owners that the site of theirs is protected by website hosting provider. So, offering them susceptible to cyber-attacks. A number of the primary key techniques and tools utilized for website security are site checking in addition to malware removal, website plan firewall, application security testing, etc.

8. Endpoint security

This allows organizations to protect the servers of theirs, mobile devices & workstations from remote and local cyber-attacks. Since products on a method are interconnected, it tends to make entry points for threats and vulnerabilities. Endpoint protection effectively secures the device by blocking attempts created accessing these entry points. File integrity monitoring, anti-malware software programs as well as antivirus, etc. Are big methods employed.

Types of Cyber Security tools

1. IBMQRadarAdvisor and Watson

This is undoubtedly the absolute best protection program used by companies. Watson, using artificial intelligence (AI), is self-learning and self-evolving telephone system. Just what it is able to be, prior to actually the chance is detected, it eliminates the section. The operating goes as such: IBM QRadar tracks the place. It gathers information and links online, offline, and within the unit with that code. It formulates a technique to add it next when an event is raised; it eliminates the chance. This is of all the absolute best web incidents? Kill security plans being used.

2. Wireshark

It is among the most popular community analyzer protocol. It assesses the vulnerable regions on the device in which the individual is working. Wireshark can collect or perhaps view the minutes of the info in addition to activities that are going on a product. The incoming and outgoing packets of info along with the protocol that's being employed in the transmission could be viewed. Just what it is able to be captures the lifestyle info and in addition, creates a traditional analysis sheet that should assist in tracking.

3. Cryptostopper

It is among the best tools on the net right now to prevent the ransomware or perhaps malware attacks on merchandise. What crypto stopper does is it finds the bots which are encrypting the documents along with deletes them. It creates a design or perhaps a deception way of the chance to latch it on by itself upon the device, when it latches itself; crypto stopper detects in addition to deletes that code. Cryptostopper makers have an inclination to produce a promise of a nine-second threat detection and also elimination challenge. It isolates the workstation along with the affected areas of the unit so that the ransomware cannot manage to affect progressively more areas.

4. N MAP

It is of all the countless primary and also open source utilities created for community securities. NMAP is not just great with very little but large networks too. It recognizes the hosts and the receiver on a product. Along with it, furthermore, it uses the distributions of operating systems. It's in a position to scan hundreds and thousands of devices on a process in one moment.

5. Burp Suite

It is another web scanning algorithm security program, which allows you to browse online uses. The main reason behind this specific gadget is checking and also penetrate the jeopardized approach. It checks the surfaces which might be influenced along with the sender along with destination's responses as well as requests for the risk. If any threat is found, it's in a position to either be quarantined or might be eliminated.

6. OpenVAS

A utility of Nessus, but fairly unique from Nessus and Metasploit though they do precisely the same, but unique. It is viewed as most likely the most stable, less loophole, and use of web security tools on the net at the next.

You are going to find two primary components of OpenVAS.

Scanner: It experiences the insecure areas as well as directs a compiled report of the majority of it with the supervisor of its.

Manager: It compiles the requests which are obtained from the scanner, and after that, it is able to make a report of all of this type of incidences.

7. Nessus

Nessus is but one additional unit which checks for malicious hackers. It goes through the pcs on the device for unauthorized hackers who try to make use of the info coming from the net. Generally, it is believed that Nessus scans for unauthorized access for 1200 times. Apart from others, it doesn't make assumptions that distinct ports are simply set for web servers as Port 80 is set for Web Server only. And also, it is an open-source unit, which provides an insecure patching assistance center, which further helps in giving achievable methods because of the affected areas.

8. Metasploit Framework

Created by Rapid7 in Boston, Massachusetts. It is considered the best open-source framework, which is utilized for checking vulnerabilities. It is a command shell as it works within UNIX; therefore owners are competent to work the hand of theirs along with automobile guidelines to take a look at along with run the scripts. Metasploit Framework has a couple of built-in, too as a few final party interfaces, which could be used to exploit the affected areas.

9. SolarWinds Mail Assure

It is a multi-functional application that addresses the vast majority of the email security issues. It is information from nearly 2 million domains, which is coming from 80 5 nations. It is the same made available as Software as a Service (SAAS). It is able to assist in the defense of the user's applications from spams, viruses, phishing, and malware.

There are plenty of other net protection tools out there that could help in eliminating the opportunity together with the above-mentioned list. They are as follows:

- Aircrack-ng

- Call Manager

- MailControl

CHAPTER - 3
IMPROVING YOUR SECURITY

Securing a Wireless Network

Therefore, it is crucial for people to learn how to protect their wireless networks to ensure their confidential information does not fall into the wrong hands. This chapter will give a brief introduction to securing a personal wireless network and how to do it. For most of the examples, NETGEAR routers will be used. If users have a different router, keep in mind that some things will be different.

Encryption

Let us begin by discussing basic encryption. Encryption, when regarding data movement over a network, is the process by which plaintext is converted into a scrambled mixture of characters. This decreases the probability that the information that was sent over an encrypted network is being used for malicious purposes. As for encryption regarding wireless routers, it is the process by which an encrypted authentication key is produced every time the correct login credentials are entered, allowing access to the network. In simpler terms, every time a user logs in to a secured router, a unique key is generated, which allows access to that internet connection.

WPA

Wi-Fi Protected Access or WPA is a security tool that was developed to replace WEP security. There are two types: WPA and WPA2. The difference is that WPA2 is a newer, more secure version of WPA. Anytime users have to log in to a wireless network, whether it's at their house or at school, they are most likely, logging into a WPA/WPA2 encrypted network. These security features work by checking whether or not the login credentials entered are accurate, and if they are, an encrypted authentication key unique to that very login is generated. Once this key is generated, it is checked by the corresponding network, allowing the transmission of data to start, assuming the login credentials were a match. Now that we have seen the basics of WPA encryption, we will discuss some basic steps that can be taken to secure personal wireless networks.

Wireless router credentials

When a wireless router is first set up, it is very important that the default login credentials are changed. Most personal wireless routers come with a standard login username and password such as:

Username: admin

Password: password

Hackers know these default login credentials, meaning, it is crucial that they are changed right away. Using a lengthy password with a combination of characters, both upper and lower cases will give users reliably secure credentials.

Service Set Identifier

A Service Set Identifier (SSID) refers to the computer language for the name of a wireless network. For example, the University of Arizona's wireless network is known as 'UAWifi.' It is important to change the name of a personal network from the default, as hackers may target a wireless network with a default name, thinking it is less secure. To further improve security, SSID broadcasting can be turned off. This means that the network will not be visible to outsiders. It will still be there, and if the specific SSID is searched for, it can be found. However, anyone scanning for a network to connect to won't be able to see this hidden network. This is especially useful when you have neighbors who are trying to gain access to your personal network.

Media Access Control

Media Access Control (MAC) is a set of numbers used to identify a specific device. Every device, whether it's a computer, tablet, or phone has an unique MAC address. To better protect a network, the router can be set to only allow specific MAC addresses to connect to that network. This adds another layer of security to your network by only permitting specific devices to connect. While this is a useful security feature, it is important to at least mention that there are software programs available that allow hackers to fake MAC addresses, allowing them to pretend to be the same device that's on your network.

The last tip we have for securing a router is the most effective method of keeping personal networks secure, turn the router off. If you're going on vacation or you simply won't be using their network for an extended period, turning off the router is the best way to avoid hackers from getting into the network. They cannot access something that is not powered on and transmitting data.

Securing Mobile Devices

This chapter will explain the security risks mobile devices face and how to better protect your data on mobile phones or tablets.

Security risks

There are three main security risks for mobile devices: physical theft, internet theft, and application permissions.

Physical theft

The physical theft of a device can allow a person to

access the device and snoop through all personal information that was stored. That could be anything from passwords, text messages, photos, emails, and so on.

Internet theft

This applies to any data stolen or seen while browsing the internet on a mobile device, whether it's on a wireless network or a mobile carrier service.

Application permissions

This is probably the biggest security threat to mobile device owners for one simple reason. People do not read what permissions an application has when downloading the app. Business Insider published a recent study which found that in 2017, 90% of consumers accepted legal terms and conditions without reading through them. This is where the security risks come into play.

The basics

Listed below are six methods that can be used to better protect mobile device security. These are up-to-date operating systems, app privileges, geo-tracking awareness, lock screens, Wi-Fi or Bluetooth safety, and internet browsing.

Operating systems

An operating system is the basis of a mobile device that manages all networks and Software. For example, Apple uses iOS, while Android uses

Android OS. Maintaining up-to-date Software for all types of mobile operating systems aid in keeping a mobile device safer. As the developers of these operating systems learn of security flaws, they are patched, and an update is sent out worldwide. This is one of the easiest methods to protect yourself from upcoming malicious Software or security weaknesses.

Applications

We all love apps, whether they come from the Apple Store or the Google Play Store, but what most people do not know is the information these apps can access via a user's mobile phone. Most people never bother to read the fine print when they are downloading the new Candy Crush game or when they're updating their Instagram app. Therefore, phones are incredibly easy targets for hackers.

Many applications request far too much data from a phone, which may not even be related to the app's actual purpose. For example, in Candy Crush's license agreement under section 10, it clearly states that the developers may use any personal data collected in any way that follows their privacy policy. They also go on to state that if users link their account to a social media site, they will use all personal data available from those sites as well to identify the user.

Geo-tracking

Most mobile device users have absolutely no idea how frequently their locations are being pinged and stored in a company's servers. Many free applications available for download in the Apple Store or Google Play Store are not actually free. There is a growing trend among app developers to collect your location using your phone or tablet's GPS system, this is known as geo-tracking. This information is gathered in huge quantities and is bought by large business entities who utilize this data to study and accurately predict consumer behavior.

Advertisers are always looking for new ways to capture your attention so that you will buy their product. If an app developer collects GPS locations from an individual on a daily basis, he or she could look at it and say, "Wow, this person seems to drive by a certain store every day." This app developer then takes this information and sells it to the store that the individual in question drives by every day so that the individual can be targeted with advertisements. These advertisements could come in the form of emails or spam text messages. How can these stores know how to direct ads at specific individuals? The answer to this is that more than just the individual's location data can be used for marketing. This app developer could have permissions that he or she will gain access to the phone's personal information like contacts, emails, etc. This allows the app developer to not only sell an individual's daily transit routes, as well as the information needed for advertisers to reach them specifically.

Passwords

This is one of the easiest methods to protecting data on a mobile phone. A simple lock screen password can prevent someone from gaining access to your phone or tablet if it is stolen. Think about all the applications, text messages, emails, and photos that are on a person's phone or tablet. Then think about someone being able to access all that information without even needing a password.

Wi-Fi safety

To avoid hackers seeing information sent from a user's mobile device, the user needs to be careful when using Wi-Fi. According to Lawyers' Professional Indemnity Company (LAWPRO), here are some tips on how you can do this:

1. First and foremost, only use wireless networks that are known and trusted. Avoid public wireless networks altogether, if possible. Public networks are usually not secure, making it easy for someone on the same network to pick up the information you sent.

2. If using a public network is a must, login to a Virtual Private Network (VPN) to secure the data you are transmitting. A VPN works by sending

encrypted data through a tunnel that is safe from being accessed by anyone on the same network.

3. Make sure the network being used is running some form of WPA encryption. Most home company networks run WPA2 encryption, unlike public networks which have no security at all.

4. If you're connected to a network that isn't your own, make sure that the device sharing settings are turned off to avoid unknown devices from connecting with yours. This creates a link between devices designed to share data easier. However, this is also an effortless way for a hacker to connect to the user's device.

Bluetooth safety

1. Most Bluetooth capable devices are shipped by the manufacturer in unprotected mode. Also known as 'discovery mode.' This mode allows the device to be seen by others, making it easier to connect with.

2. If you are not using your Bluetooth, make sure to turn it off to avoid any connections to other unwanted devices. Turning your Bluetooth off when it's not in use eliminates all chances of an attacker's device connecting to yours.

3. If possible, change your device settings, so it requires user confirmation before it pairs with

another device. This eliminates the possibility of another device secretly connecting.

4. Do not connect to unknown devices. Only pair with devices that are known and trusted.

5. The maximum range of Bluetooth connections can differ based on the power of the device itself, and by setting the range to the lowest possible setting, the risk of an attacker reaching the device is reduced.

Internet browsing

1. Internet browsing can still be dangerous, even on an iPad. Here are a few dos and don'ts from the McAfee Security Advice Center when it comes to surfing the web on a mobile device:

2. Install antivirus software, if possible, to run scans on any downloaded content on your device.

3. Always look at the URL of the web pages you visit. Make sure that you check the https security feature.

4. Fake websites tend to have some errors ranging from the overall look of the page to improper grammar.

5. If the URL of the website you wanted to visit is known, enter it directly to avoid any possible fake copies of the website.

6. Avoid clicking on advertisements as these can

lead to malicious websites designed to install dangerous Software on your device.

CHAPTER - 4

ENHANCING PHYSICAL SECURITY

Early Detection is the Game Changer

The Study on Global Megatrends in Cybersecurity, sponsored by Raytheon and independently conducted by Ponemon Institute, provides new insights into the most critical cyber-threat trends emerging over the next three years through the eyes of those on the frontline of cybersecurity.1

More than 1,110 senior information-technology practitioners around the world were surveyed.

The study revealed key insights and predictions from the expert practitioners for the next three years, such as:

Cyber extortion and data breaches impacting shareholder value will increase.

- 67 percent said the risk of cyber extortion, such as ransomware, will increase in frequency and payout.

- 60 percent predicted state-sponsored attacks would become even worse.

- Only 41 percent said their organization would be able to minimize Internet of Things (IoT) risks.

The frequency of cyber extortion, nation-state attacks, and attacks against industrial controls were predicted to increase by double-digits.

- 19 percent said cyber extortion is very frequent today, while 42 percent said this threat would be very frequent over the next three years.

- 26 percent said nation-state attacks are very frequent today, while 45 percent said this would be very frequent over the next three years.

- 40 percent said attacks against industrial controls and supervisory control and data acquisition (SCADA) systems are very frequent today, while 54 percent said this would be very frequent over the next three years.

The loss or theft of data from unsecured Internet of Things (IoT) devices is likely to happen and is a significant cybersecurity challenge.

- 82 percent said it is very likely, likely, or somewhat likely that their organization will have a loss or theft of data caused by an unsecured IoT device or application.

- 80 percent said likelihood of a security

incident related to an unsecured IoT device or application could be catastrophic.

In summary, Raytheon and Ponemon Institute's Study on Global Megatrends in Cybersecurity provides several predictions from cybersecurity practitioners across the globe, who are on the frontline defending against the cyber attackers daily. Among them, over the next three years, even with all of the increased spending on cybersecurity:

- Cyber extortion and data breaches will greatly increase in frequency. This trend will largely be driven by sophisticated state-sponsored cyber attackers or organized groups.

- IoT devices, in particular, are very susceptible and will be targets that will be exploited.

- So, it is not a question of IF, but WHEN the cyber attackers will break-in. And when the cyber attackers break-in, they will remain undetected for many months.

- The median or mean number of days the cyber attackers remain undetected varies based on the source. Examples are:

- Mandiant's M-Trends Report;

- Verizon's Data Breach Investigations Report;

- IBM and Ponemon Institute's Cost of a Data Breach Study.

One thing is certain, however. The cyber attackers are able to hide for many months, and the longer it takes to detect the cyber attackers, the more the cost the organization ends up suffering.

Based on a research into dozens and dozens of cases, I have identified signals in the Cyber Attack Chain that every organization should understand and look for.

When researching the cases, it became evident that in each case, the cyber attackers took steps that fit into one of the steps as I have outlined in the Cyber Attack Chain. It was also clear that in each step, there were signals of the cyber attackers at work, but that these signals were not detected by the organization.

It is time for every organization to understand what the Cyber Attack Signals are, and implement them as part of their cybersecurity program. By doing so, they will transform the defense into offense and detect the cyber attackers early.

A Cyber Attack Signal is a high-probability signal of cyber attackers at work, trying to hide and avoid detection, while performing one of the tasks in the Cyber Attack Chain. They are at work to accomplish their ultimate objective—the theft of data or intellectual property (IP) or other compromise, harm, or disruption. A Cyber Attack Signal focuses on cyber attackers' behavior.

I have identified 15 Cyber Attack Signals that, as a minimum, every organization should focus its monitoring on. These Top 15 signals relate to cyber attackers' behavior. They are timely signals, before the cyberattack is executed, occurring at the intrusion, lateral movement, or command and control steps of the Cyber Attack Chain, and are, therefore, of greatest value.

This is not an exhaustive list, and there will probably be other signals relevant to an organization based on its risk profile and its Crown Jewels that may indicate the cyber attackers at work. As such, each organization should tailor its list of Cyber Attack Signals for monitoring.

Intrusion

Patch window

This is the time period a vulnerability remains unpatched and also how attackers could exploit it, providing an alert about Crown Jewels possibly impacted, probable attack timeline, and expected attacker behavior.

Web shell

This is the attempted installation or installation of a web shell to a web server. It would exploit server or application vulnerabilities or configuration weaknesses to make the intrusion.

Lateral movement

Abnormal logons

These are anomalies in logons compared to normal logon patterns.

Privileged users' behavior

These are anomalies in the behavior of privileged users (users with greater access levels and capabilities) compared to normal behavior.

WMI anomalies

This is an abnormal activity with Windows Management Instrumentation (WMI), a set of tools for system administrators to manage Windows systems locally and remotely.

Internal reconnaissance signals

These are anomalies in scripts or batch scripts running on email, web and file servers or domain controller or hosts, or scanning of servers and ports.

Malware signals

These are anomalies from normal behavior patterns in terms of users, files, processes, tasks, sources, and destinations to indicate initial malware installation or propagation.

Ransomware signals

This is anomalous activity to indicate initial ransomware installation or propagation, such as the installation of new .dll file or attempted communication with a TOR website (i.e., server on the TOR network, a service used to provide anonymity over the Internet.)

Malicious PowerShell

This is an abnormal activity with PowerShell, a scripting language for system administrators to automate tasks, such as odd characters (e.g., + '$ %) added in the scripts, use of "powershell.exe" by abnormal users at unusual times or locations or scripts containing command parameters.

RDP signals

These are anomalies with Remote Desktop Protocol (RDP), which enables a user (e.g., as help-desk staff) to use a graphical interface to connect to another computer in a network, such as abnormal RDP users, source or destination logons.

SMB anomalies

These are anomalies with Server Message Block (SMB), a protocol in Microsoft Windows that enables remotely managing files, file sharing, printing, and directory share, among other functions in a network.

Unusual logs behavior

These are anomalies in event logs, such as event logs removed, stopped, or cleared with details (user details, date, time, type of log, the command executed, asset impacted, source, and destination).

Command and control

C&C communications

This is anomalous activity indicating attempted communication or communications with a command and control (C&C) server, such as a request to an unusual domain name or a one-off domain name, a request to the numeric IP address as the domain name for the host, requests to certain IP addresses or hosts with a certain frequency (hourly, daily or other).

ICMP packets

These are anomalies with Internet Control Message Protocol (ICMP) packets, such as abnormal size, frequency, source, or destination.

Hidden tunnels

These are anomalies of HTTP, HTTPS r DNS traffic compared to normal baseline patterns indicating communications with a C&C server using a tunnel designed to blend in with normal traffic.

CHAPTER - 5

SECURING YOUR SMALL BUSINESS

Computer and Network Security

As the internet has evolved over the past decade, so have hackers. Network security has become one of the most crucial factors companies consider because of the continuous growth of computer networks. Big corporations like Microsoft are constantly designing and building software products that need to be protected against hackers and foreign attackers because these are the kinds of people who will stop at nothing until they get what they want. The more network security an individual has, the less chance there is of a hacker accessing their data and files.

Network security is the process by which measures are taken to prevent unauthorized access, misuse, or modification of information passed over a network. In other words, network security simply means that any computers accessing a private network are protected from any forms of cyber theft or manipulation.

Network security

There are three ways to better protect a network; these are intrusion detection systems, WPA/WPA2, which stands for 'Wireless Protected Access,' and Security Sockets Layer (SSL).

Intrusion Detection Systems

These systems are software pr0grams designed to protect networks. They are intended to monitor server channels and detect malicious programs being sent across these servers. There are two types of IDS systems. The first is known as an active IDS, this is a more secure software that not only monitors server channels, but it can also block and remove any malicious programs it detects. This type of IDS system doesn't need human involvement to protect a computer or network. The second kind of IDS is less protective in that it only monitors a server and alerts a user to a threat if one is found. These programs will not destroy or quarantine any malicious software.

Wireless Protected Access

Wireless protected access, also known as 'WPA,' is a form of network encryption. There are two types of this security system, WPA, and WPA2. Both are more secure than the traditional WEP security found on old routers, and WPA2 is the most secure. Most modern routers found in stores today offer

WPA2 encryption levels. The reason why both security features are useful is because they make it more difficult for an attacker to get into a wireless network. WPA2 offers a higher and more complex security layer by using different key setups for network access. This means that WPA2 makes it harder for an attacker to crack a password for a wireless network.

Security Sockets Layer

A Security Sockets Layer (SSL) is a form of internet protection provided by encryption. Its purpose is to encrypt any data you send over a network to prevent anyone else on your network from seeing the actual information being transferred. SSLs are very important for anyone entering private information on a website. They work by verifying what is known as a website certificate. A certificate is what websites use to verify themselves. When you connect to a website, the server the website runs on sends you its certificate to verify its authenticity. A website can only acquire these certificates by applying for them, and they have to follow a strict set of security guidelines.

So, to keep this from getting complicated, if a website has a credible website certificate using SSL, any information you send or receive from that site will be encrypted and safe from any possible attackers.

Also, you can see if a website is secure by looking

for the https in the URL at the top of your internet browser.

Computer security

Computer security, on the other hand, is the protection of data physically stored on a computer. This includes taking steps to prevent attacks under the triad of information security, also known as the CIA (confidentiality, integrity, and availability).

A few of the basic methods below pertain to computer security and will cover passwords, software updates, firewalls, anti-virus or malware programs, ad-blockers, email encryption, and data backups.

Having a good password

A good password consists of three basic qualities: Its length, the characters used, and the combination of upper- and lower-case letters. The longer a password is, the harder it is to break. Some hackers try to use algorithms in which they send massive amounts of combinations, hoping that one is a match to the secret password. By increasing the length of a password, its chances of being cracked decreases.

A mixture of letters and symbols, such as exclamation marks, help protect your password from being stolen. This also applies to add uppercase letters into your password. A password such as 'password1' is very weak in comparison to a password like 'PasSWord2018!' The combination of upper-case letters and symbols decreases the chances that a password can be hacked through brute force.

Another method you can use to create incredibly secure passwords is getting a program like 'LastPass' or 'Password Boss.' These programs randomly create a password that is incredibly secure. Using a program like this will provide a unique password for everything a person uses. This means that if a hacker can get into one of an individual's accounts, they will not have the password for the other programs or web services.

Software updates

Software updates are very important as they protect your computer or mobile device. Software updates are used to patch holes or bugs found in an operating system, and this will make your device more secure. Check your operating system often to see if a new update is available. Some operating software update automatically.

Firewalls

Firewalls are great protection for computers because they prevent unwanted data from getting to your computer. They monitor the flow of incoming data and run checks to see if the information that's about to be received by your computer is harmful or not. For example, anytime a user downloads something from a website, the firewall will scan the file in question and determine if it is malicious or not. Not all firewalls are the same. Most operating systems come with a built-in firewall, so there is hardly a reason to install additional firewalls. Also, these OS companies are constantly updating their security features to make them more reliable. Firewalls prevent unauthorized access to or from a private network.

Antivirus software

One of the most effective and common methods of dealing with malware is anti-malware Software. Programs such as Windows Essentials, McAfee, and Bitdefender allow a user to run scans on a system to search for infected files. If any files are found to be corrupted, these programs alert the operator, allowing him or her to remove the files in question. This type of Software is also very useful as it can scan any downloaded items or email attachments before allowing the user to download them. This is a crucial protective barrier, as it prevents any malicious programs from installing itself on a device.

These types of Software can also analyze what kind of virus, worm, or Trojan has infected the computer in question. This kind of protective Software will remove anything malicious automatically from the computer but will be unable to recognize threats such as ransomware or keyloggers.

Ad blockers

Most browsers have extensions that can be added to the browser, which blocks pesky advertisements. For example, the Google Chrome web store has a variety of additional extensions users can download and run while using the browser (not all being adblockers). Chrome has an adblocker made specifically for the Chrome browsers, which limit the number of ads that pop up while you visit websites. Ad blockers can also be downloaded directly onto the computer's hard drive instead of a web browser.

Email encryption

Encryption protects emails by making the content of emails unreadable to any entity, besides the intended recipients. Popular email services such as Gmail have since added encryption of emails to their network. However, it only protects data that's on their servers. This means that data is still vulnerable while it bounces around on other internet networks unless users implement client-side encryption. Most methods that allow this are complicated processes that require exchanging certificates with everyone who will be receiving or sending emails with one another.

Fortunately, there is an alternative called Virtru that works with Gmail accounts as well as Outlook. This allows users real, client-side encryption without the prolonged process of exchanging certificates.

Virtru is a plug-in that users can download onto their web browsers to freely send and accept emails from Outlook or Gmail accounts without any compatibility issues.

Data backups

Data backups are an important but overlooked aspect of computer security. By performing regular backups of all important data on a computer, the user protects themselves from the risk of a crash or virus and lose important data. Data backups typically upload data to an outside source, either to a cloud storage server, or a storage device. Any data that isn't backed up can be completely lost if the computer hardware fails or data is corrupted. Like the old saying, "It is better to be safe than sorry."

Failed security

If both security types fail, what could be put at risk? The types of information hackers may attempt to steal are divided into two categories: personal and financial. Regarding personal information, a hacker could use it to create fake web accounts, social media accounts, or a new identity altogether. The rampancy of identity theft today is fueled by the enormous amounts of information that can be collected from the internet. According to the identity protection service LifeLock, in 2017, 16.7 million people were victims of identity theft, resulting in $16.8 billion being stolen. In 2016, 15.4 million people were victimized, resulting in a loss of $16.2 billion. Over the past three years, the number of people who are victims of identity theft increased by 3.6 million.

With financial information, it all comes down to the individual's money. A hacker can use the stolen financial information to make online purchases, apply for loans, or go as far as to file tax returns under the victim's name. It is of the highest importance that both types of information remain protected and accurate.

According to the USA government, there are several diverse types of identity theft that the general public could fall victim to:

Child ID theft

Child identity theft is a type of theft that can go hidden for many years until the child has grown into an adult. By then, the damage to their identity from the theft has already been inflicted.

Tax ID theft

This occurs when a social security number is stolen and used to file tax returns by anyone other than the owner of the SSN.

Medical ID theft

This type of theft occurs when someone steals another person's medical information or health insurance data for medical services, or by billing false charges to the policy holder's company.

Social ID theft

Known nowadays as a 'catfish,' this kind of theft happens when someone steals another person's name, photographs, and other personal information to create a fake social media account.

CHAPTER - 6

MALWARE

Let's imagine a scenario where a client presents a file, and they are unsure if it's malware and what capabilities it has.

Where does this malware fit in the kill chain?

Is it the initial patient zero machine that will go online and download more malware code? What is this malware's specimen capability?

Understanding what the malware is capable of is one of the main purposes of malware analysis or reverse engineering. You also have to ask: What is the attacker's intention?

If it's malware specifically for ransom, they are trying to encrypt for files and ask for money. If its purpose is to install other stolen PI data, then its intention is larger than just quick financial gain. Knowing the intention of the attacker helps you understand where else this malware is infecting your environment.

Types of Malware

Malware is a very general category, and there are few subtypes within it:

Ransomware

This malware is designed to freeze files and, as the name suggests, demand ransom from its victims in exchange for releasing the data; successful attackers realized that they could take it a step further by demanding money but not releasing the data. Instead, attackers demand another payment, and the cycle continues.

Paying up might seem like the only solution to dealing with ransomware, but the fact is, once you pay, the attackers will keep asking for more.

Adware

This is Software that downloads, gathers, and presents unwanted ads or data while redirecting searches to certain websites.

Bots

Bots are automatic scripts that take command of your system. Your computer is used as a "zombie" to carry out attacks online. Most of the time, you are not aware that your computer is carrying out these attacks.

Rootkits

When a system is compromised, rootkits are

designed to hide the fact that you have malware. Rootkits enable malware to operate in the open by imitating normal files.

Spyware

Spyware transmits data from the hard drive without the target knowing about the information theft.

Remote Access Tool (RAT)

After your system is compromised, RAT helps attackers remain in your systems and networks. RAT helps criminals to obtain your keystrokes, take photos with your camera, and/or expand to other machines. One of the most dominant features of this type permits the malware to transfer all of this information from the victim to the attacker in a protected way, so you are not even conscious you are being spied on.

Viruses

A virus pushes a copy of itself into a device and becomes a part of another computer program. It can spread between computers, leaving infections as it travels.

Worms

Similar to viruses, worms self-replicate, but they don't need a host program or human to propagate. Worms utilize a vulnerability in the target system or make use of social engineering to fool users into executing the program.

CHAPTER - 7
CYBER ATTACKS

Web Attacks

SQL Injection

SQL injection is also called as SQLI. SQL is a particular type of attack which uses malicious code for manipulating backend databases to attain data that was not wished-for display. Such data may consist of various items such as private customer details, private data of the company, and user lists.

SQLI can cause destructive effects on a business. An effective SQLI attack can result in the deletion of complete tables, unsanctioned inspecting of user lists, and in few cases, the attacker can attain administrative access to a database, making it extremely destructive for a business. While calculating the expected price of SQLI, we must take into consideration the loss of customer faith in personal case information of the customer, such as details of credit card details, addresses, and phone numbers are stolen. Even though SQLI can be employed to attack any SQL database, the criminals frequently target websites.

Cross-Site Scripting

Cross-site scripting (abbreviated as XSS) is a type of injection breach where the criminal transmits malign code into content from otherwise trustworthy websites. Such incidents take place when an uncertain source is permitted to attach its own (malign) code into different web applications, making the malign code bundled together with other content, which is then directed to the browser of the victim.

Attackers normally send malign code in the form of fragments of the JavaScript code implemented by the browser of the victim. The exploits consist of malign executable scripts in various languages such as HTML, Java, Flash, and Ajax. Cross-site scripting attacks can be extremely destructive; nonetheless, dealing with susceptibilities enabling such attacks is comparatively simple.

Distributed Denial-of-Service (DDoS) Attack

The aim of Denial-of-service (DDoS) is to shut down a service or network, making it unreachable to its intended users. The attackers attain their aim through crushing the victim with the traffic load or else flooding it with data, which activates a crash. In both circumstances, the DoS attack denies genuine users like account holders, and company employees.

The targets of DDoS attacks are often web servers of prestigious organizations like government and trade organizations, commerce, media companies, and banking. Even though such attacks don't lead to theft or loss of crucial data or other assets, still such attacks can cost the target loads of time and money to mitigate. DDoS is frequently employed in combination to divert from attacks of another network

Password Attack

A password attack is an effort to obtain or else decrypt the password of the user with maligned intentions. Different techniques are used by crackers such as dictionary attacks, password sniffers, and cracking programs in password attacks. Even though there are some defense mechanisms against such attacks, however normally, the method used is to inculcate a password policy which comprises a minimum length, distorted words, and frequent alterations.

The recovery of the password is generally carried out by the continual guessing of the password by using a computer algorithm. The computer repeatedly tries various combinations until the successful discovery of the password.

Eavesdropping Attack

These attacks initiate with the interference of network traffic. Another term used for Eavesdropping breach is sniffing or snooping. It is a type of a network security attack where the attacker attempts to steal the data send or received by computers, smartphones, or other digital devices. Eavesdropping attacks are hard to detect as they do not cause anomalous data transmissions.

Eavesdropping attacks aim at faded transmissions amid the server and the client, which allows the attacker to obtain network transmissions. Different network monitors such as sniffers on a server can be installed by the attacker to implement an eavesdropping attack and intercept data. Any device which is inside the transmission and reception network is a vulnerability point, including the initial as well as terminal devices. One method to guard against such attacks is having the information of devices connected to a specific network as well as information about software running on such devices.

Brute-Force and Dictionary Network Attacks

Brute-force and dictionary attacks are networking attacks in which an attacker tries to log into account of the user through systematically checking and exasperating all likely passwords until he finds the correct one.

The ordinary way to carry out this type of attack is through the front door, as we must have a technique of logging in. If we have the necessary credentials, we can enter as a normal user without arising doubtful logs, or tripping IDS signatures, or requiring an unpatched entry.

The meaning of brute-force is to overpower the system via repetition. During password hacking, the brute force needs dictionary software, which combines dictionary words with hundreds of diverse variations. This process is rather slow. Brute-force dictionary attacks can make 100 to 1000 attempts per minute.

After trying for numerous hours or even days, such attacks can finally crack any password. These attacks restate the significance of best practices of passwords, particularly on critical resources like routers, network switches, and servers.

Insider Threats

An attack doesn't need to be always performed by someone from outside an organization. At times, malicious attacks are carried out on a network or computer system by any individual sanctioned to access the system. Insiders executing such attacks have the advantage over outsider attackers as they have authorized system access. Moreover, they are most likely to understand network architecture and system policies.

Additionally, normally there is minor security against insider attacks as the focus of the majority of organizations is to defend themselves against external attacks. Insider threats can leave an impact on all elements of computer security. Such attacks can range from injecting Trojan viruses to thieving private information from a system or network.

Man-in-the-Middle (MITM) Attacks

Man-in-the-middle (abbreviated as MITM) attacks are a kind of cybersecurity breach permitting an attacker/cracker to eavesdrop a communication amid two bodies. The attack takes place amid two genuinely communicating parties, allowing the attacker to capture communication, which they otherwise should not be able to access. This gives such attackers the name "man-in-the-middle." The invader "listens" to the communication through capturing the public key message transmission and then retransmits the key message whereas switching the demanded key with his own.

The two communicating parties continue to communicate routinely, without having any idea that the person who is sending messages is an unknown criminal who is trying to alter and access the message prior to its transmission to the receiver. Therefore, the intruder in this way controls the whole communication.

AI-Powered Attacks

The idea of a computer program learning on its own, constructing knowledge, and becoming more sophisticated in this process sounds scary (Adams 2017). We can easily dismiss artificial intelligence as another tech buzzword. Nevertheless, at present, it is being used in routinely applications with the help of an algorithmic process known as machine learning. Machine learning software aims to train a computer system to carry out a specific task on its own. Computers are trained to complete tasks by repeatedly doing them, whereby getting knowledge about particular hindrances that could hamper them.

Hackers can make use of artificial intelligence to hack into various systems such as autonomous drones and vehicles, altering them into prospective weapons. AI makes several cyber-attacks like password cracking, and denial-of-service attacks, identity theft, automatic, more efficient and powerful. AI can even be used to injure or murder people, or cause them emotional distress or steal their money. Attacks on a larger scale can affect national security, cut power supplies to complete districts, and may shut down hospitals as well.

CHAPTER - 8

CYBERWAR

Consider an employee's W-2 form. Before the 2000s, the information on this form had a nominal value that approached the price of the paper on which it was printed. There was no easy way to monetize a stolen W-2 form. Today, there is a thriving black market for personally identifiable information. As of 2017, the going price for a W-2 is between $4 and $20, depending on the income of the wage earner. That may not seem like much, but it represents a massive increase from the two-cent value of a printed W-2 decades ago. Stealing even a single W-2 makes sense when attackers operate from a country where $20 is a full day's wages. Stealing them by the hundreds or thousands using automated attacks against scores of unsuspecting and unprepared small businesses makes even more sense for criminals anywhere in the world.

Having established why hackers are coming for your data, let's look at the damage done when they strike. Continuing with the W-2 theft example, state and federal laws require employers to report cyber theft, also known as a data breach. Failing to disclose the breach opens the door to class-action lawsuits where juries can award unlimited damages to victims due to your negligence. Disclosing the breach helps shield you and the organization from claims of negligence and, in some cases, will prevent class-action suits. However, the organization will not be off the hook completely. Defending a non-class action lawsuit will cost tens of thousands of dollars, even if you win.

Additional costs include losses the employee will suffer if their identity is used to open credit in their name, drain their bank accounts, etc. Worse, the threat of identity theft will follow them forever. Related, indirect costs to the employer include replacing the employee if he or she quits and a reduction in morale among peer employees. It may become harder and more expensive to hire good talent, and customers hearing of the breach may look at competitors they believe are more vigilant.

A single stolen W-2 might net an attacker $20, but your organization and employees may be on the hook for tens or hundreds of thousands of dollars in damages. And this is just one example of how cyber-attacks wreak havoc on an organization. Black markets and cyber espionage make seemingly mundane data worth stealing and exploiting. Trade secrets, access to bank accounts, and private communication are very lucrative targets. Sometimes it is not your own data, but a client's data accessible through you or your employees that is the target.

Our highly connected, the digital world has ushered in a new era of cybercrime. One that is growing fast and changing constantly. Executives who stick their heads in the sand, try to keep a data breach a secret, pass off cybersecurity as just an IT problem, or wait for government protection will pay a steep price.

Many executives in the 1990s were adamant that computers were a novel expense that would never add real value to their business models. The idea that they would elevate the discussion of computers to an executive-level was as absurd as typing their own email. Executives that clung to this view doomed their company to lose ground when competitors with forward-thinking executives raised technology to a boardroom discussion. Today cybersecurity is what computers were then. It is history, repeating itself, and we already know who wins. Organizations led by executives that are willing to buck old-school thinking and grapple with the Wild West of cybersecurity will come out on top.

Today, the outdated view is thinking that cybersecurity is a technical problem best delegated to information technology (IT) experts. It goes hand-in-hand with the idea that cybersecurity involves only preventing attacks by anticipating them and implementing as many deterrents as possible. In contrast, a modern view of cybersecurity recognizes that countering every possible attack to achieve perfect security is financially unfeasible. This new mindset also considers what happens when attacks occur, because they will. Astute executives realize that spending every dime on prevention is futile and take a more holistic view of the problem.

Finding the right balance among various preventive and preparatory measures is like building an investment portfolio of stocks, bonds, and real estate. The right mix depends on what the external markets are doing and your appetite for taking risks. As time goes on, the markets will change, and your life circumstances change. Allocations in your portfolio adjust accordingly. This book is a guide to making investments in cybersecurity that reflect the external threat landscape, internal business strategy, and the organization's appetite for risk.

Despite having excellent cybersecurity teams and multi-million-dollar budgets, large companies have learned that cybersecurity is a business problem that must be managed from the top. They have realized that outsourcing and delegation only go so far when building a comprehensive cybersecurity plan and keeping it up to date as internal and external circumstances change. For the foreseeable future, the management of cybersecurity as a business problem will rest upon the shoulders of top management. Unless you embrace this new role, your organization will be a cybersecurity have-not in a time where data privacy and security are of increasing concern among clients and suppliers.

What happens if you do not step up to the plate? Well, according to a 2017 report, nearly one-quarter of small businesses that suffered a ransomware attack were forced to immediately stop their operations. How long can your organization survive if revenue-generating operations stopped abruptly while payroll and other expenses continued? What will long-term damage be done to your clients' perception of your organization's ability to offer uninterrupted service?

Savvy competitors simply wait for your market share to open up as a result of your inattention. On the flip side, effective management of cybersecurity is necessary just to stay on par with forward-thinking competitors. Having a comprehensive cybersecurity plan in place can position your company to survive the same attacks that will bankrupt (or severely disrupt) your peers. When that happens, you can pick up their market share and grow your company.

Another reason to take cybersecurity seriously at the executive level is that larger, cyber-savvy companies are often direct, or indirect, clients who take the security of their supply chain very seriously.

Studies show that as many as 63 percent of data breaches are linked to a third-party because weak downstream suppliers make great back doors into otherwise secure systems. In response to this, the NIST Cybersecurity Framework (a technical implementation guide) was recently revised to add emphasis to supply chain scrutiny, and an executive order from the White House drove this same point home for government agencies. The government, their downstream contractors, and large private sector companies will begin culling lax suppliers and awarding business to those who demonstrate they take cybersecurity seriously. Nimble executives who address cybersecurity at their core will have an advantage—one that differentiates a company from its competitors and may command a premium. If you insist that your plate is full just managing what you already have, you will miss the opportunity to rise above your competitors, just like the old-school executives who refused to see technology as anything more than an expense.

Consumers have also become quite sensitive to cybersecurity, and it is reflected in their buying habits. Forward-thinking executives can capitalize on this trend too. A prominent example was Apple's stance on personal privacy when the FBI demanded they decrypt an iPhone used in a terrorist event. Playing up their investments in encryption and demonstrating loyalty to a client even in the worst of times helped solidify consumer trust in Apple products. We would never advocate brinksmanship with the FBI, but Apple's response was a brilliant way to gain confidence among consumers. Learning to manage cybersecurity from a business perspective means you can spot and leverage opportunities like this too.

CHAPTER - 9
ETHICAL HACKING

When it comes to security, being a hacker is one of the most commonly used terms. It appears everywhere, and even the entertainment industry and many authors often use it in their movies, books, TV shows, and other media forms. Therefore, the word "hacker" is usually seen as a bad profession and always associated with dark or real criminal activity. So, when people hear that someone is involved in hacking, they immediately see that person as someone who has no good intentions. They are usually presented as "operators from the shadows," even antisocial. On the other hand, they are also seen as a social activist. This label became especially popular after a few things like WikiLeaks. Many hackers were involved in obtaining many important documents from governments, politicians, and companies that showed information that was very different from the information given to the public. Organized groups such as Anonymous or Lizard

Squad have also had a huge impact on the hacking experience in recent years.

Examples: Mischief or Criminal?

- Hacking is by no means a phenomenon that has appeared overnight. It existed in various forms and evolved all the way from the 1960s. However, it was never tackled as a criminal activity at first. We'll look at some cases that will take a closer look at some of the attacks, and generic examples that have gradually changed that picture.

- Access services or resources that you do not have permission to use. This is usually called stealing usernames and passwords. In some cases, obtaining this information without permission is considered a cybercrime, even if you do not use it or as accounts of friends or family members.

- There is a form of digital offense called network intrusion that is also considered a cybercrime. In essence, as with ordinary offenses, this means that you went somewhere without permission to enter (or in this case, access). So, in case someone gets access to a system or group of systems without permission, we can say that the person violated the network and thereby committed cybercrime. However, some network intrusions can take place without using hacker tools. Sometimes logging in to guest accounts without prior permission can be seen as cybercrime.

- One of the most complex yet simplest forms of hacking is to go after the most vulnerable element in the system—people. This type of cybercrime is known as social engineering, and we say it can be simple because the person is a much more accessible part of the system than any other, and it's easier to deal with. However, people can provide clues that are difficult to understand, whether spoken or not, making it difficult for the hacker to get the information they need.

- The issue of posting or sending illegal material has generally become difficult to address, especially in the past decade. Social media received a lot of attention, and many other internet-related services increased in use and popularity. This allowed many illegal materials to move from one place to another in the shortest possible time, allowing it to spread very quickly

- Fraud is also common, especially on the internet, and is also considered a cybercrime. Like the original term, fraud in cyberspace also means that a party or parties have usually been misled for financial gain or harm.

What does it mean to be an ethical hacker?

All the things we mentioned earlier in this chapter referred to hackers in general. The real goal, however, is to learn how to be an ethical hacker and explore the skills you should have.

Ethical hackers are people who are usually employed by organizations to test their security. They usually work through direct employment or through temporary contracts. The key is that they use the same skills as all other hackers, but there is one big difference: they are allowed to attack the system directly from the system owner. In addition, an ethical hacker means that you reveal the weaknesses of the system you have evaluated (because every system in the world has them) only to the owner and no one else. In addition, organizations or individuals hiring ethical hackers use very strict contracts that specify which parts of the system are authorized for an attack and which are prohibited. The role of an ethical hacker also depends on the job to which he or she is entitled, i.e., the needs of the employer. Today, some organizations have permanent staff teams, and their job is to conduct ethical hacking activities.

Hackers can be divided into 5 categories. Keep in mind that this format may vary, but we can say these are the most common:

- The first category is also referred to as "Script Kiddies." These hackers usually have no training or do, but very limited. They know how to use just some of the basic hacking tools and techniques, and since they are not competent enough, they may sometimes not fully understand their activities or the consequences of their work.

- The second category concerns hackers known as "White Hat hackers." They attack the computer system, but they are the good guys, which means they don't harm their work. These types of hackers are usually ethical hackers, but they can also be pentesters.

- "Gray Hat Hackers" are the third hacker category. As their name suggests, they are between good and bad, but their final decision is to choose the right side. Still, these types of hacker's struggle to gain trust because they can be suspicious.

- The fourth category we mention in this section is referred to as the "Black Hat Hackers." This category refers to the hackers we mentioned earlier in this chapter. These people usually work on the 'other side' of the law and are usually associated with criminal activities.

- Last but not least are the "Suicide hackers." They are called that because their goal is to prove the point, which is why they want to take out their target. These hackers don't have to worry about getting caught, because their goal is not to hide, but to prove, so that they are easier to find.

Responsibilities of an Ethical Hacker

The most important thing that an ethical hacker should learn and never forget is that he or she should always have permission for any kind of system attack. The ethical code that you, as an ethical hacker, must implement in every task says that no network or system should be tested or targeted if you do not own it or if you do not have permission to do so. Otherwise, you may be found guilty of multiple crimes that may have occurred in the meantime. First, it can hurt your career, and second, if it's something really serious, it can even threaten your freedom.

The smartest thing is to get a contract from your employer the moment you test or attack the required target. The contract is a written authorization, but you should keep in mind that you should only examine the parts of the system specified in that contract. So, if your employer wants to give you permission to hack additional parts of the system or remove authorization for some, he should first change the contract and you shouldn't continue working until you get the new permit. Note that the only thing that distinguishes an ethical hacker from the cybercriminal is the contract. Therefore, you should always pay special attention to the vocabulary related to privacy and confidentiality issues, as it often happens that you come across intimate information from your client, both business and personal.

That's one more reason why your contract should include who you can talk to about the things you found while researching the system and who are forbidden from hearing updates from you. In general, customers usually want to be the only people who know everything you eventually find out.

An organization known as the EC Council (International Council of Electronic Commerce Consultants) is one of the most important organizations when it comes to regulating these issues. According to them, an ethical hacker should keep all information obtained on the job private and treat it as confidential. This is indicated in particular for the customer's personal information, which means that you are not allowed to transfer, give, sell, collect or do any of the customer's information, such as social security number, etc. -mail address, home address, unique identification, name, and so on. The only way you can give this type of information to a third party is by having written permission from your employer (client).

While some may argue about the distinction between hackers and ethical hackers, the division is quite simple: hackers are separated by their intentions. This means that those who plan to harm and use their skills to access data without permission are labeled as black hats, while those who work with their client's permission are considered white hat hackers. Naming these two categories of "the bad" and "the good" can be controversial, so we'll try to follow these expressions in the following way:

- Black hats usually operate outside the law, which means they do not have permission from the person called "the customer" to consent to their activities.

On the contrary, white hats have permission and permission from the person called "client," and they even keep the information they have between client and white hats only.

Gray hats, on the other hand, enter both areas and use both types of action in different periods.

Hacktivists are a category of hackers that we have not mentioned before. They belong to the movement known as Hacktivism, which refers to action's hackers use to influence the general public by promoting a particular political agenda. So far, hacktivists have been involved with agencies, large companies, and governments.

Hacker Ethics and Code of Conduct

Like any other profession, hacking has its Code of Conduct that establishes rules that can help customers (individuals or organizations) evaluate whether the person who interacts with their networks and computer systems is generally reliable. The organization that implemented this Code has already been identified and is known as the EC Council. Obtaining a CEH reference from the EC Council means that you fully understand the expectations you must meet. We've provided some parts of the code, so make sure you read it and get familiar with it.

- Information you gain during your professional work should be kept confidential and private (especially personal information)

- Unless you have your customer's permission, you may not give, transfer or sell the customer's home address, name, or other unique identifying information.

- You must protect the intellectual property, yours and others, by using skills that you have acquired yourself so that all benefits go to the original creator.

- Be sure to disclose to authorize personnel any danger that you suspect may be from the Internet community, electronic transactions, or other hardware and software indicators.

- Make sure that the services you provide are within your area of expertise so that you work honestly while aware of any limitations that may be a result of your education or experience.

- You may only work on projects for which you are qualified and carry out tasks that match your training, education, and work experience skills.

- You must not knowingly use software that has been obtained illegally or has been stored unethically.

- You may not participate in financial practices that may be considered misleading, such as double billing, bribery, etc.

- Make sure you use the customer's property properly, without exceeding the limits set in your contract.

- You must disclose a potential conflict of interest to all parties involved, especially if that conflict cannot be avoided.

- Make sure that you manage the entire project you are working on, including promotion and risk disclosure activities.

CHAPTER - 10

MISTAKES MADE IN CYBERSECURITY

Stolen information and data will not lead to the end of the business. It is not a great sign for the business either. Studies and research indicate that a data breach in an organization's network can lead to a loss of $15.4 million, and the amount increases each year. People do not want to lose their money because of some issues or vulnerabilities in the system, do they? Indeed, businesses and organizations cannot make mistakes. These mistakes can lead to the loss of data, but a large organization is bound to make such mistakes. What the organization must do is to learn from those mistakes. You cannot expect your organization to do the exact thing repeatedly only because the outcome may change at one point. This chapter covers the different mistakes organizations make. You must protect your organization from making such mistakes during these times.

Failing to Map Data

Every organization must focus on understanding how and where the data flows. It should also look at where the data is saved. Remember, data is the livelihood of your company. It is only when you assess and identify the flow of data that you can see where it must be protected. You must know if the data is flowing out of your organization and who it is shared with. When you have visibility, you will know what ends the hacker can attack. You will also know where you can catch the hacker.

Neglecting Security Testing

Vulnerabilities will reside across the database, systems, applications, and network. These vulnerabilities now extend to various devices like the IoT or Internet of Things and smartphones. Organizations must test these devices and connections regularly to scan for any vulnerabilities. You can also perform some penetration tests to learn about the vulnerabilities. Remember, you cannot guess the vulnerabilities, and will only find them when you test them.

Concentrating on Wrong Aspects

It is true that prevention is not an anachronism. As technology advances, so make the threats against it. Remember, a hacker will find a way to enter the border. A firewall will not always protect your systems if you have an employee who does not know what he is doing. Once a hacker is inside the system, he can acquire privileged information. He can also pretend to be an employee of the organization. Hackers can evade any security scans for a long time. If you have better visibility, you can find a hacker and reduce the chances of data leaks.

Forgetting the Basics

Often, it is the simple things you can use to overcome and threats to the system. You must train all your employees. Help them understand the type of password they must use. They must perform the right actions as well. It is only when this happens that you can maintain the network components properly and minimize the risk of data loss. You can also find ways to configure the data to prevent any changes adequately.

Avoiding Training

Remember to train your employees to know what they must do to prevent any attacks. The most common form of hack is a social engineering attack. The hacker will send information from a malicious source and mask the information to seem legit. He can then use the information the employee feeds into the website, and attack the configuration of the system and network. Make sure to train your staff about protecting their systems and how to identify social engineering attacks.

Security Monitoring

Most businesses cannot set up their security operations center or center of excellence since they lack the budget. This does not mean you cannot monitor the security of the systems and network. You must investigate the network and look for any threats or vulnerabilities. You can use these methods to minimize the effect of an attack on the data and security.

Avoiding Vendor Risk Assessments

From earlier, you know vendor risks are the reasons for numerous data breaches. Hackers can enter the organization's systems through the vendor's application or network. Therefore, you must have a plan to help you assess the risks in third-party systems. You can also read the reports they share about their systems to learn more about their security.

Ignoring Shadow IT

Remember, the end-points in any network are often connected to other networks, and this makes it hard to control the flow of data through the network. Most employees access shadow devices and applications from their laptops and desktops. The IT department in most organizations does not support the use of such applications. If you do not know how to stop it, you must find a way to hide it. You can block these applications and websites.

It is not only about Malware

Most hackers use malware to establish their presence in a system or network. Once they are inside the network or system, they will use different strategies to perform the hack and move through your network. So, you need to find hack into the system in a legitimate way and perform the hack to detect any vulnerabilities.

Breaches won't Happen

This is one of the biggest mistakes most companies make. Some organizations do not protect their business and network since they believe cybercriminals do show mercy. This is never going to happen. Cybercriminals will attack any company, regardless of its size. You must prepare your defenses and identify the response to an attack. This will help you minimize the damage and react faster to any threats if the day does come.

Forgetting about the Management

You must understand that security must mature over time, and this is one of the primary objectives of an information security professional. In some instances where businesses have reached high levels of maturity, security is a part of the organization's culture. You must obtain permissions and approvals from the management before you investigate any attacks or the systems.

Doing it on Your Own

Regardless of whether you own a small business or are a part of a larger organization that lacks security skills, you must find someone to help you with testing your network and systems. Hire an ethical hacker to test the networks and systems. You can also partner with security service providers. Alternatively, you can speak to your management and hire the right professionals, or you can train the employees in your firm.

You must avoid making these mistakes if you want to improve the security of your organization's systems and networks.

Tips to Keep Your Organization Secure

In this chapter, we will look at some tips to help you protect your organization from being a victim. Speak to the IT professionals and other stakeholders in the business to learn more about what you can do to prevent any cyber-attacks.

Creating an Information Security Policy

Every business must have a clearly defined security policy. This policy should provide information on the processes and actions every employee in the organization must follow. You must enforce this policy and train employees to perform the right actions. Remember to include the following in your information security policy:

- Best Practices for encryption
- Password requirements
- Usage of devices
- Email access

You must update this policy frequently, and let every employee in the organization know about the changes made to the policy.

Educating Employees

This is a very important aspect to consider. If you have a security policy, but your employees do not know what they must do, then it is a lost cause. Help your employees understand the different protocols they must perform. You need to have the training and let people know what they must do. This is one of the easiest ways to protect data.

Using Secure Passwords

Remember, passwords are important to maintain cybersecurity. Instruct your employees to choose passwords that are difficult for a hacker to guess. You must avoid the usage of dates and names in your password since hackers can easily connect you with those words. You must also instruct them to change passwords regularly. You can also use a multi-factor authentication system to add an extra layer of protection to the accounts.

Ensure Software is Updated

If you have outdated software in your systems, it can lead to a security risk. You should always update the software with the latest patches. For example, if you use the Windows Operating System, you must allow the updates to run so that you can cover any vulnerabilities or gaps.

Secure the Network

You must use firewalls to protect the network used in the system. Make sure to use encryption, so you make it harder for a hacker or any other user to access the data. You must be careful when you use Wi-Fi since most hackers target those connections. Let employees know they should not use public Wi-Fi. Ask them to use VPN connections to secure the transmission of data. Make sure to protect the router using a strong password.

Back-Up the Data

Regardless of how vigilant you are, a hacker can choose to target your system or network. Store the data on a disk in the event of such an attack. Let the system store the data automatically in a secure place. You could also store the data in a separate data center.

Control Access

You must ensure to maintain some control over the devices used by employees as well. Employees must be careful about the information on their screen, and should never leave it unlocked. If they leave their station or desk for a minute, they must log out of that system. Since anyone can walk away with a laptop, employees should be told never to leave it unattended. Since more business is conducted on tablets and smartphones, hackers target these devices. Employees must secure their data on the phone and protect their phones using a password. They must report the loss or theft of the device promptly.

Cybersecurity Training

Organizations can always reduce the risk of cyber-attacks by training their employees. They can use Target Solutions Cybersecurity Training for employees. This training material will provide dynamic courses to check the user's knowledge about cybersecurity.

CHAPTER - 11
ECONOMIC IMPACT OF CYBERSECURITY

The Business of Cybersecurity

Funding higher levels of cybersecurity is part of the business problem executives must address. Small and medium businesses often operate on razor-thin margins. Therefore, it is important to ensure every cybersecurity dollar is spent wisely. Failure to do so not only leaves gaps in security, but overspending can destroy a competitive edge on cost. When allocating funds, it is important to decide which cybersecurity expenses are treated as a cost of goods sold and which to consider as investments for improving profits and winning market share. It is the same problem executives faced during the rise of computers and the Internet decades ago: "Is this newfangled stuff to be treated as an expense or an investment?" We argue that it is both and will help you understand both perspectives.

It is particularly hard for busy leaders of small

companies to prioritize risk management planning. They want to jump to the part where they buy cybersecurity solutions and get back to running their business as quickly as possible. Taking time to think about strategy, for a small company, seems like a waste of time when there are customers waiting to be served. But nothing could be further from the truth, and we also understand that it can be daunting to think about cybersecurity when everything is so technical. We use the terms strategy and tactical to identify those areas that need your attention and which to consider delegating or outsourcing.

Before we dive into our step-by-step explanation of your role, let's examine several of the contributions and benefits to executive involvement. Most of these functions are impossible to outsource because they require expertise and authority that only top management possesses. That doesn't mean you cannot use tools and advisors to help you along the way; it just means you cannot relinquish responsibility for them.

Stating and controlling direction. Goal setting starts at the top and reflects the needs of the business. Goals and objectives provide context for tactical planning, and communicating them clearly to a diverse team of expert tactical advisors keep everyone focu5sed, and on the same page.

Allocating budget. Business owners understand

that cybersecurity measures will cost time and money, and as an executive, it is your responsibility to decide where the money will go. Your IT guru recommends a new firewall. Then your insurance agent recommends adding a cyber insurance policy. If you buy both (and you should buy both), how do you divide up the limited budget between all the possible solutions? If cybersecurity is relegated to just a tactical IT problem, you will have a fantastic firewall but no protection when a hacker finds their way around it.

Authorizing company-wide policies. Whether it's enforcing bring-your-own-device policies or using strong passwords, someone should be in control of what's being done and how well policies are being followed. The ability to authorize new cybersecurity measures comes from the top in any organization. The people-driven aspects of cybersecurity are absolutely a business problem that you, as the top manager, need to oversee.

Maintaining compliance. Once authorized, policies and procedures must be carried out. Failure to do so will be construed as negligence, which leads to prosecution and regulatory fines. Cyber insurance, citing "failure to follow" exclusions, will also deny coverage if you fail to maintain your own security standards. Your authority and your ability to develop a culture of compliance are critical to avoiding these catastrophic mistakes.

Empathy in a crisis. When a data breach happens, despite every effort to prevent it, clients and employees will be more forgiving if they believe top management was paying attention and making an effort. Even when responsibility for a breach can be traced to an individual or external actor, clients and employees want to know that you were being vigilant.

Justify spending. The return on investment for cybersecurity is obscured. It is hard to measure how bad things could have been if you did not invest in something that prevents or reduces loss, but that does not mean it is impossible. Risk management tools and techniques that have been adapted to cybersecurity can rationalize spending. Whether you report to yourself or another stakeholder in the company, you can invest with confidence when you can articulate the value.

We will not go deeply into tactical details that can be delegated to staff and vendors, although we will explain what they are and how they get used so you can manage them effectively.

Bonus: How to Stop Identity Theft on Facebook and Other Social Media

Sharing is a core value of social media and a key reason for the wild growth and success of companies such as Facebook, Twitter, YouTube, and LinkedIn. For some of us, it's fun to post comments, articles, photos, and videos for our friends and social media followers. Many people participate passively, watching, and reading others' posts but rarely sharing their own. Never have humans had such open and easy access to tell their personal stories or share their ideas, experiences, and feelings.

But like much about the Internet, all this sharing can draw unwanted and dangerous attention. You don't want the "bad guys" watching you. And any social media platform you use potentially connects you to mind-boggling numbers of people. Over a billion people worldwide have a Facebook account2, 307 million people actively use Twitter3, and the number of Instagram users exceeds 500 million. 4 That's why you must exercise complete control over your digital life, and you do that on social media by keeping a sharp eye on your privacy settings. Nearly all social media sites let you control who sees your information. When you review your privacy controls regularly, you ensure that you have the strongest security in place.

Who Can See Your Profile?

Social media networks continue to grow and allow you to connect with family, friends, colleagues, and classmates, but sharing without thinking about who sees your information just invites trouble.

We often ask people we meet if they've checked their social media privacy settings lately—many have no idea. That usually means the public can view their open profiles—posts, photos, likes, friends, and other activities. You may be OK with that openness, but you should be concerned.

Scammers can "scrape" or copy your profile, learn more about you, and use that information to perpetrate any variety of scams, frauds, and hacks. For example, say you post a photo of your dog in your backyard and write a caption such as "Look at Buddy soaking up the sun." A scammer who reads that post now has a good chance of answering the password reset question on your email account if you selected: "What's your pet's name?" An open profile gives hackers the important details they need to hack your life—whether it's seizing your email account, assuming your identity in credit-card fraud, or cracking your bank account. 5 Strong privacy settings block hackers from seeing your profiles.

Know Your Privacy Settings and Your Friends

You can still enjoy social media and maintain good security; you just need to strike the right balance by knowing how privacy settings work at different sites. A simple Google search on a website's name and "privacy settings" will get you started. All social media sites will give you some measure of control over who sees your profile and activities. Your biggest decision will be selecting a security level that allows you to share with friends while keeping your privacy. Thankfully, it won't involve much effort.

In addition to beefing up your privacy settings, you'll also need to review your "friends" to make sure you still want them to see your social media activities. For example, should the friend of a friend know when you are on vacation because they can see your photos? It's important to remember that your posts have a larger audience than you realize. Also, social media companies frequently change their privacy policies and default settings. Pay attention to privacy updates you receive from Facebook and other sites: They're not just "fine print" and often contain important changes that need your attention if you want to keep strong privacy on social media.

We think most people should follow this rule: Do not leave your profile open for everyone to see. A study by antivirus firm Norton found that four in every ten social media users have suffered fraud.6 Open profiles essentially hand over your personal information to scammers and hackers without much effort. Don't make their job easy. Think twice about what you share and with whom—a key rule to hack-proofing your life.

CONCLUSION

The United States has complained that Russian hackers had meddled with the 2016 presidential elections. It was a major incident. Russian hackers hacked into Democratic National Committee and published some pretty confidential emails during the 2016 presidential elections in the United States. This episode produced quite a stir in the legislative corridors of the United States. The power and impact of cybersecurity were revisited, and the importance of cybersecurity was elevated, and for the first time, cybersecurity was seen through the context of international relations. The incident was not normal as it had the potential to push the two countries into a kind of conflict. The level of the attack was unprecedented in nature, not only in the United States but also across the globe. People had started seeing cybersecurity from a different lens. The incident of Sony Pictures started spinning before the eyes of lots of people who responded with mixed sentiments. Some of them showed a bit of surprise, and others showed extreme concern, while a few showed no reaction at all.

The United States had accused a state of cyberattack in the past in the wake of the attack on Sony Picture Entertainment, but the scale and the impact of this attack were unprecedented. It meant that anyone with a computer could change the course of an election of the most powerful country in the world. But for seasoned cybersecurity experts, this development is not news. Since the advent of the internet back in the mid-1990s, the cyberspace has witnessed some pretty amazing growth that filled the pockets of millions of people due to rapid commercialization but also pushed people into the depths of the crisis. Cybersecurity has now climbed up the ladder and has reached the heads of the state who have started seeing the security of the world in a different way. Scholars of international relations see this new discipline as a subfield of security studies with a special focus on the implications of technology for international security. This takes into account its effects on the sovereignty, power, and world governance.

Cybersecurity has gained considerable attention for the past few years on the back of the fact that the attacker is usually not known. This creates a lot of confusion and suspicion that are very unhealthy for a peaceful international environment. Large nations sometimes use proxies to wage cyberattacks and afterward label them as a rogue to avoid direct confrontation with the power they are dealing with. We have seen this in the North Koran attack on Sony Pictures. North Korea denounced the attack by appreciated their deed as patriotic. Similarly, when the Russian hackers meddled in the US elections, Vladimir Putin, the Russian president, denies any involvement of the state in the attack but added to the tail of his speech that some patriotic minded Russian hackers might have committed that deed. He appeared to have been appreciating what the hackers had done to the country that had a long history of enmity with Russia.

Had Putin claimed the attack, there would have been an all-out war between the two superpowers of the world. Cybersecurity is playing a crucial role in international relations because the threat of nuclear war and the mutual assured destruction as a result of the war have negatively affected the world's strategic scenario. Humans, by nature, cannot live without a contest. Physical war is not possible as the threat of nuclear war keeps looming over the participants of the war. We can see this in the subcontinent where India and Pakistan, the two nuclear powers, have made the subcontinent a nuclear flashpoint in the area. Despite the fact that the possibility of a conflict remains high, the idea of a hot war is not usually pursued by the two countries. So, if countries must go into a conflict, they choose the cyber realm to fight each other. Cyberwarfare is an advanced mode of cold wars. I have quoted the example of a scenario in which India responded with a hacking attack after the Pulwama attack. Similarly, North Korea attacked Sony Pictures through a cyber-security breach because it didn't have the power to confront the United States, and also it had to give a befitting response to Sony Pictures for making the movie that was a spoof of an assassination attempt on Kim Jong-un.

Cybersecurity issues are becoming more lethal day by day, and it remains doubtful that it will help improve international relations. Up till now, it has shown great potential in complicating and destroying international relations.

This book has explained all the necessary details on the subject of cybersecurity. You have learned what the basics of cybersecurity are. You have also learned what the general motivations are behind an act of cybercriminal. I have discussed in detail was social engineering is and how it is used by malicious hackers to infiltrate a facility. Then I moved on to explain cyber terrorism, its types, and its adverse effects on the modern world, such as the relations between countries and the general peace of the country.